Tropical Rain Forests

by Libby Romero

Table of Contents

Introduction

A tropical **rain forest** is a special place. Millions of types of plants and animals live in rain forests. In this book you will learn about tropical rain forests.

Words to Know

adapt

canopy

emergent layer

forest floor

habitat

rain forest

tropics

understory

See the Glossary on page 22.

3

Chapter 1

What Are Tropical Rain Forests?

A tropical rain forest is a warm, wet **habitat**. It is full of plants and animals. Tropical rain forests are in the **tropics**. All tropical rain forests are near the equator.

tropical rain forest

4

The Amazon Rain Forest is the biggest rain forest in the world. It is in South America.

Amazon
Rain Forest

VENEZUELA
GUYANA
SURINAME
French Guiana
(French colony)
COLOMBIA
ECUADOR
Amazon River
PERU
BRAZIL
BOLIVIA
PARAGUAY
URUGUAY
ARGENTINA
CHILE

What Are Tropical Rain Forests Like?

Tropical rain forests have four layers.

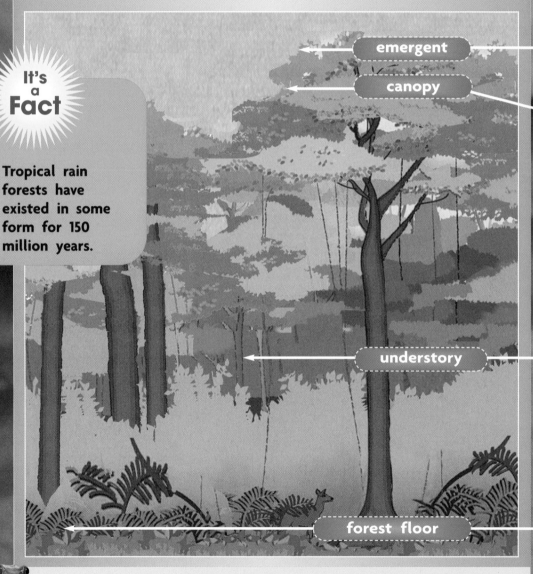

It's a Fact

Tropical rain forests have existed in some form for 150 million years.

emergent

canopy

understory

forest floor

▲ the four layers of a tropical rain forest

The **emergent layer** is on top. Tall trees grow out of it. The **canopy** is like the roof of a tropical rain forest. The **understory** is filled with young trees and shrubs. The **forest floor** is very dark. Not much sunlight gets here.

It's
a
Fact

It is easy to walk through rain forests. Rain forest floors do not have many plants.

Tropical rain forests are always wet! They can get up to 400 inches (1,016 cm) of rain each year.

Tropical rain forests do not get cold. It is usually between 68°F (20°C) and 86°F (30°C) in a tropical rain forest.

MATH CONNECTION

Solve ┼ This

(Hint: To find the average, first add the 5 temperatures together. Then, divide by 5.)

		thunderstorms		
mostly cloudy	sunny	thunderstorms	scattered thunderstorms	scattered thunderstorms
High: 94°	High: 92°	High: 91°	High: 89°	High: 88°
Low: 72°	Low: 72°	Low: 69°	Low: 68°	Low: 66°

Read the 5-day weather forecast for Rio Branco. Rio Branco is in Brazil's tropical rain forest. What is the average high temperature for these 5 days?

What is the average low temperature?

Answer: average high: about 91°; average low: about 69°

There are other types of forests in the world. Most people live in areas with deciduous forests. Leaves fall from deciduous trees in winter.

	Tropical Rain Forest	Deciduous Forests
Location	around the equator	between North Pole and tropics, between South Pole and tropics
Rainfall	at least 80 inches (200 cm) a year	30–60 inches (76–152 cm) a year
Temperature	average 80°F (27°C)	average 50°F (10°C)
Plants	huge trees, vines	deciduous and evergreen trees, shrubs
Animals	monkeys, jaguars, birds, large snakes, insects	squirrels, rabbits, birds, deer, bears, snakes, insects
Daylight	lasts for 12 hours a day all year long	more daylight in summer than in winter

▼ tropical rain forest

▼ deciduous forest

9

What Lives in Tropical Rain Forests?

Millions of different kinds of plants and animals live in a rain forest. Mammals, lizards, and reptiles live in a rain forest. Insects live in a rain forest.

Ants are almost everywhere in a tropical rain forest. ▼

Did You Know ?

Some scientists study insects in the rain forest. The scientists spray a natural chemical on the canopy. Insects fall to the ground where the scientists can study them more easily.

▲ Howler monkeys live in the canopy.

Animals live in all four layers of the rain forest. Most animals live in the canopy.

Learn More

You can visit http://www.sci.mus.mn.us/sln/tf/s/strata/strata.html to learn more about tropical rain forests.

▲ Jaguars live and hunt on the forest floor.

The biggest animals live on the forest floor. Some of these animals can climb trees.

Rain forest animals are just right for the rain forest. They are just right for their habitat. Being just right is being **adapted**.

Toucans crack hard seeds in the rain forest with their beaks.

toucan

▼ Sloths use strong claws to climb rain forest trees.

Many plants live in rain forests. Some rain forest plants do not grow in the ground. They hang from trees.

Orchids grow on trees to reach the sunlight in the canopy.

Did **You ?** Know

Some rain forest plants can live outside the rain forest. People grow them inside their houses!

13

Many plants and animals need one another to survive. This plant grows high on trees. Then it can reach sunlight.

The middle of the plant catches rainwater. Insects and small frogs can live in this rainwater.

Chapter 4

Why Are Tropical Rain Forests Important to Us?

▲ Rain forest trees recycle much of the air we breathe.

Earth needs rain forests. Rain forests are important in world weather patterns.

Scientists also use rain forest plants to make medicines.

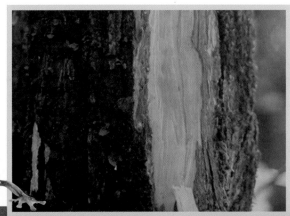

◀ Bark from this rain forest tree cures many illnesses.

Rain forests give us many foods. Bananas, avocados, and pineapples first grew in rain forests. Oranges and coffee beans first grew in rain forests, too.

bananas   avocado   pineapple   orange   coffee beans

Humans are the biggest threat to rain forests. We cut down trees for wood. We cut down plants to grow farm crops.

Learn More

You can visit
http://mbgnet.mobot.org
to learn more about the
importance of rain forests.

Some people live in rain forests. They have learned to survive without harming the land.

People to Know

Chico Mendes worked hard to protect the Amazon Rain Forest. You can learn more about this rain forest hero at this Web site:

http://myhero.com/myhero/hero.asp?hero=j_muir

Click on the picture of Chico Mendes to read about his life and death.

Rain forests are full of life. It is important to protect the rain forests.

Summary

Rain forests are important to Earth.

Tropical Rain

weather

- warm
- always wet

chapter 1

layers

- emergent
- canopy
- understory
- forest floor

chapter 2

Forests

life

- plants and trees
- people
- animals

chapter 3

human uses

- food
- wood
- medicines

chapter 4

 **Think About It**

1. What does a tropical rain forest look like?

2. Why are tropical rain forests important?

Glossary

adapt just right for a habitat

*Some plants **adapt** to get more sun and water.*

canopy the second-highest layer in a rain forest

*Treetops make the **canopy**.*

emergent layer the highest layer in a rain forest

*The tallest trees grow out to form the **emergent layer** in a rain forest.*

forest floor the bottom layer in a rain forest

*Jaguars live and hunt on the **forest floor**.*

22

habitat the place where special plants and animals live

*The rain forest is a warm, wet **habitat**.*

rain forest a warm, wet area with special plants and animals

*It rains almost every day in the **rain forest**.*

tropics the warm, rainy areas near the equator

*The weather is hot in the **tropics**.*

understory the third layer in a rain forest

*The **understory** of the rain forest is formed by the leaves of young trees and shrubs.*

23

Index